THE HEARTBEAT OF THE FATHER

Kholofelo Kolanisi (Madam K)

The Heartbeat Of The Father

To _____

From _____

Date _____

Kholofelo Kolanisi (Madam K)

Unless otherwise identified: All scripture quotations, are taken from the New King James Version (NKJV) of the Holy Bible.

The Heartbeat Of The Father

ISBN: 978-0-620-86974-4

Published by:

Graceworx Publishers, Pretoria

23 Bureau Lane

605 Centenary Building

Church Square, Pretoria

0817677828

Content Layout & Cover Design:

Graceworx Publishers

CONTENTS

Introduction

'm writing this book amidst the pressure of bowing to the word that has been spoken upon my life and lots of postponement, procrastination and sheer laziness or perhaps unbelief.

I remember one of the things Jesus rebuked his disciples was unbelief and I guess sometimes when walking with God, you falter, fall and get back again.

I will not claim to be perfect but I believe I am being perfected and becoming more like him and this book, that is long-awaited by a lot of people is finally being birthed.

Today is the 10th of June 2015 and finally, I have decided to start typing what has been embedded in my spirit. This day is very important to me personally because it is my birthday and this book is being birthed at the exact day that I was born and I believe it is not in any way a coincidence.

I would like to thank the Holy Spirit right now for being my teacher and helper in birthing what God has put in my heart concerning this book.

This book is titled the heartbeat of the father which is a message that kept on coming in bits and pieces and I believe the Holy Spirit will continue to speak throughout this book until it is completed.

The first bit came through a painful experience that I don't wish to experience ever in my life. It was a roller coaster experience where I saw and heard God speaking through first-hand painful experience.

It all started when my sister was rushed to the hospital to give birth to her third son. Though it was an emergency, all seems to be going well but that was the beginning of the roller coaster.

She had to undergo a cesarean section and the baby had to be quickly drawn out. I'm intentionally using the word drawn out for a reason to be explained in later.

After what looked like a rushed operation, finally, the baby arrived and unfortunately after some serious resuscitation and Doctors fighting to bring him back to life, he could not take the first breath and eventually the Doctor, taking off his gloves and with that face you don't want to see when you have a loved one at the hospital finally went to my brother in law to announce that they have lost the baby.

It was a blow, disappointing and more so for my sister who will now have a scar for life to remind her what she has lost.

As if that was not enough, now the hospital was following the procedures of how to prepare for the corpse and filling in the appropriate forms, to everyone's surprise, the baby decided to start breathing on his own. No machine, no nurse, no doctor, absolutely no human hand or experience, just the hand of God he breathed and continued to breathe.

Can you imagine the excitement and the jubilee within the family? I for one was over the moon. I immediately went to the hospital where we had a prayer and from that short prayer God spoke to me about Isaiah 9:6 and to the father of the baby, he deposited John 10:10 and that was where the names Bophelo and Matete came about, one meaning Life (from John 10:10 and another meaning Wonder from wonderful counsellor from Isaiah 9:6.

Later that day, another Pastor and Prophetess, we call her Mama Zee, called them and just asked how the Isaiah 9:6 baby was doing. And to us, that was a confirmation about the names given to the boy and the celebration just couldn't stop.

They say I'm generally the vibrant and loud in the family (though I believe I'm very shy and quiet) compared to my sister and I went on a rampage shopping for the little one and I was unstoppable. You see, Khutso is my one and only sister so in a way I still see her as my younger sister despite her being a married woman and a mother herself there is still that younger sister for me.

The boy was growing very fast and started feeding on the milk and gaining weight as well. All was going accordingly now and every day was good news until the wonder boy started showing 3 fingers as the mother was taking him pictures every day.

The following day he showed 2 fingers then one finger as the days went by. Little did we know what the fingers meant until it was rather too late for us to interpret.

We went to the hospital after bible study to encourage and pray with my sister and during prayer, I saw the names of the boy written on a stone, like a memorial stone and that was the day when he had already shown one finger. Little did we know that the boy was making his exit as he had accomplished the message he brought.

Suffice it to say that he lived exactly 30 days from that miraculous day and as for me, each day he made a mark. Actually, in my opinion, I think some people are still alive and have lived so many days and years but have not yet made an impact like this boy had in 30 days.

It was on the last day, or rather the last hour of his life when I heard God speaking to me from the wonder boy's hospital bed. Firstly as you enter the ward, you are required to sanitize your hands, wash and sanitize every other minute before you touch him. There were so many machines around him. One on the head, stomach, nose and he was breathing from the assistance of machines and the heartbeat was monitored.

Right in the midst of all that God spoke to me about the wonder boy. The Holy Spirit brought the picture of Moses in the burning bush. Before that, he reminded me of the name Moses itself which means "drawn out of the water". I remembered how the boy had to be taken out of the water to save his life when he entered this world and God continued to say to me that when he introduced himself to Moses from the burning bush he said: "I am the God of your father Abraham, Isaac and Jacob."

From that moment onwards, as I was praying and holding his tiny hands, God continued depositing words in my spirit. He said to me, in the physical, this boy knew his father because he comes from his seed and for him (wonderboy) to understand and know God the Father, will be because of his natural father who is a wonderful man of God, called and planted in the word of God. It is through the knowledge and the intimacy of the natural father that wonder boy would understand and experience God the spiritual father. It is like what Jesus kept on saying that "If you have seen me, you have seen the father in me."

Those few hours were so profound to me because God was calling upon the fathers towards their sons, it was like some kind of reconciliation of what God's perfect plan is concerning the fathers and sons and what he has planned for us.

From that day, my life changed completely. I saw the heartbeat of the father everywhere I went. Whenever I read the bible I couldn't help but see the heartbeat of the father everywhere.

I remember when I saw the pictures of my son playing that I just started crying and missing my father so much. It was a very strange feeling for me because my parents divorced when I was still very young and those pictures made me to long for a father who could follow me around, adore me and take lots of pictures. I remembered when I shared my longing feeling of my father with a colleague she said to me, it must be God the father reminding you that he is a father to the fatherless.

That was actually far from the truth I was about to unveil in my life. The very same day my brother from my father's side, which in English you may call him my half- brother (we don't have this in Africa, we are simply brothers and sisters, no halves and quarters at all). He went to request my numbers and he called me the following day telling me that his life will not continue as if we are non-existent and that he would love to have a relationship with his sisters and I even discovered that my grandmother and my father's younger brother were still alive which brought such a light into my dark life. That longing immediately lifted as hope just shone inside of me and I just knew there was more to this heartbeat than I thought and also that God is capable of speaking in mysterious ways and through whatever circumstances.

I have learnt to listen more than talk this days and the fact that I managed to fill up just one page writing something is indeed the launching of a miracle.

CHAPTER 1

A CHILD IS BORN, A SON IS GIVEN

I would like to lay the foundation by comparing the two kinds of sons spoken about in Luke 15:1 with the son spoken about in Isaiah 9:6 and right now ask the Holy Spirit to give me the revelation as I write this passage.

Luke 15:11

11 And he said, A certain man had two sons: 12 and the younger of them said to his father, Father, give me the portion of goods that falleth to me. _And he divided unto them his living,_ 13 and not many days after the younger son gathered all together, and took his journey into a far country and there wasted his substance with riotous living14 and when he had spent all, there arose a mighty famine in that land; and he began to be in want. 15 And he went and joined himself to a citizen of that country; and he sent him into fields to feed swine. 16 And he would fain have filled his belly with the husks that the swine did eat: and no man gave unto him. 17And when he came unto himself, he said how many hired servants of my father's have bread enough and to spare, and I perish with hunger!18 I will arise and go to my father, and I will say unto him, Father, I have sinned against heaven and before thee, 19 and am no more worthy to be called thy son: make me as one of thy hired servants, 20 and he arose, and came to his father and when he was yet a great way off, his father saw him, and had compassion, and ran and fell on his neck and kissed him. 21 And the son said unto him, Father, I have sinned against heaven, and in thy sight, and am no more *worthy to be called thy son. 22 But the father said to his servants, bring forth the best robe, and put it on him; and put a ring on his hand and shoes on his feet: 23 And bring hither the fatted calf, and kill it, and let us eat and be merry.*

From this scriptures, we read of the two sons who both lived with their father. We are told that the youngest son requested his inheritance from his father and the father obliged.

We also learn that the inheritance was divided among the two sons but one of them left to a far country with his inheritance and squandered it abroad.

The first thing that caught my attention was that the son intentionally and recklessly disconnected himself from the father. Often as believers we choose to stay away from God the father or we disconnect ourselves from him to such an extent that we think we are capable of living our lives apart from Him and that we can live independent of him. We get to be too big for our boots and eventually, we realize that we need the guidance, protection and covering of the father.

It is important for the body of Christ to realize the role we ought to play amongst ourselves as one body. The body of Christ can never function fully until we realize the role we should play in people's lives. Generally, the father must understand his role and responsibilities in the lives of his children, likewise, children should understand the same.

Psalm 127:3-5

3. Behold, children are a heritage from the LORD, the fruit of the womb a reward.4. Like arrows in the hand of a warrior are the children of one's youth.5. Blessed is the man who fills his quiver with them! He shall not be put to shame when he speaks with his enemies in the gates

There comes a time in a man's life when he must rise to stand against his enemies. It is crucial to comprehend the mystery of the gates in our lives because it is at the gates where the battle takes place whenever the enemy attack, he attacks at the gates. So every man should guard and intensify gates in their live. We take victory at the gates and we also loose at the gates.

When battle arises, there is no warrior who can ever wake up and decide to go to the battle unless he is armed. A warrior should be trained, equipped and armed before going to confront the enemy. We all need to be armed for battles against our enemies.

Children are like arrows in the hand of the warrior. To take victory in every battle as the body of Christ, the heart of the father must be turned to their children and the hearts of the children to their fathers.

A quiver is a bag used to carry the arrows of a warrior for the battle. Every father has a quiver that carries arrows when he goes to the battle.

Children ought to realize that whenever the father goes to battle, they are the arrows in the quiver. Every father has a quiver, but he needs to acknowledge that he can never go to the battle with an empty quiver. A man with an empty quiver can never go to the battle. It is then imperative for the father to possess the arrows (children) when he goes out.

The father is a warrior armed with arrows (his children) for the battle. The father knows the importance of placing his arrows not anywhere but within his quiver. To overcome, the father needs his children as much as they need him.

In various gates of our lives (educational, financial, material gates...), we are defeated because children think they can succeed without their fathers likewise fathers without their children.

The principle is that children should allow themselves to be hidden in the quiver of the warrior. Only the warrior knows when to use a specific arrow. Many times we move from the presence of the father and out of the quiver of the father simply because we think we are well developed and polished enough to destroy the enemy. Children should remain in his quiver as arrows until the perfect time comes. There is no safer place for an arrow to be than in the quiver. Brethren don't just rush to go out of the quiver simply because the warrior has taken out other arrows before you.

5. **Blessed is the man who fills his quiver with them! He shall not be put to shame when he speaks with his enemies in the gates**

As much as an arrow needs to be in the quiver, the father (warrior) is blessed when he has the arrows. The father protects and polishes the arrows until the perfect time, yet the father must acknowledge that he is also blessed by the same arrow.

Over the years, I observed one area that destroyed many people in ministry and ministry itself. Where it is difficult for the warrior to release an arrow. When the arrow is polished and the time is perfect, the father must release the arrow in order for him to conquer the enemies at his gates.

Arrows are directed and release by the father to the right targeted place. The father should conquer the fear of how far will the arrow go when the time comes. When the warrior releases the arrow, the arrow always reaches to levels the warrior never reached.

If I am to put it in lay man's language, I would say that the covering of the father is like an insurance policy and disconnecting yourself from the father is like skipping your premium payments and being involved in an accident during that time. If that ever happened to you, then you know that no matter how good you were in paying your premiums, the insurance company will not even give you a second chance to explain yourself once you are involved in a car accident. In fact, before they can even process your claim, they check if your premiums payments are up to date and immediately decline your claim.

We thank God that our father is not like the insurance company. Basically what I'm saying is that, stay connected to your source to continue being like a tree that is planted by the rivers, whose leaves never run dry to produce your fruits in season.

We then saw another type of son, that is, the one who remained with the father and his inheritance yet he didn't enjoy the very blessings that came with the inheritance and the covering.

This son actually got so upset with the father that in his own words actually wished his father could have slaughtered a goat for him. Can you imagine a situation where the whole kraal belongs to you yet you settle for a goat?

How many believers today are like the second son? Born again, washed in the blood of Jesus yet still being tormented by not knowing the contents of their will long after Jesus has shed His blood and left the inheritance for them?

Hebrews 9:16 *says:* **"For where there is a testament, there must of necessity be the death of the testator". For a testament is in force after men are dead, since it has no power at all while the testator lives.**

In legal terms, a testament is a 'will' and it only comes into effect once the testator dies and you can only claim your inheritance thereafter.

Jesus already died and resurrected yet we are still oppressed by the devil. We have a loaded gun, ammunition but still fail to pull the trigger. We have a blank cheque yet we go to sleep hungry. We are bitten up, abused and desperate as if we don't serve a living God.

Beloved, I pray that we will wake up from this slumber and see what our redeemer has done for us. I pray that we can arise to the reality that we are the possessors of heaven on earth.

Romans 4:13 confirms the kind of inheritance that we possess. It says, ***"For the promise, that he should be the heir of the world, was not to Abraham, or to his seed, through the law, but through the righteousness of faith.***

We are the seed of Abraham which qualifies us to be the heirs of the world. How many of us still want to buy a piece of land to build a house when the bible says we own the land. We are masters yet we live like slaves. We are still complacent in buying what belongs to us and even rejoice and celebrate when the house is complete, throw a party on what is rightfully ours. We are still entangled in mortgage loans for years of properties that heaven says we own. We have the title deed yet we still write the offer to purchase.

I pray to God that by the time you finish reading this chapter, your eyes will open, your stronghold of imaginations will be pulled down, your feathers will be unclamped and that you will soar like the eagle that God has called you to be.

Now let's check another type of son as outlined in **Isaiah 9:6.**

For unto us a child is born, unto us a son given: and the government shall be upon his shoulder: and his name shall be called Wonderful Counsellor, The mighty God, The Everlasting Father, The Prince of peace.

Wow, what a son this is?

He is born a child but given as a son. He has big shoulders to carry the whole government.

He is a gift to the world. He is ready to carry the whole world on his shoulders.

Sometimes as believers when we go through challenges, we despise those challenges, forgetting that God does not use you until you have experience. Most powerful, anointed ministers of healing have gone through or are struggling with some kind of illness themselves, those who went through family challenges or divorce, minister powerfully in that same place where they were squeezed, crushed and all that remained was what God filled them with. In a nutshell, everyone has a wilderness experience and God likes using His people when they are in trenches.

Do you actually know that the person who gets born again is not the same person who God eventually use? Working with or for God is like seeking for employment. There is always some kind of experience to attach to your resume/Curriculum Vitae.

Do you remember David when he was about to fight Goliath? He spoke about his credentials, he remembered that he killed a bear and a lion and that was a stepping stone towards his success. The six feet tall man just became thee uncircumcised Philistine in his eyes.

1 Samuel 9:2 gives us a description of Saul and specifically says *"From his shoulders upward, he was taller than any of the people."* and **1 Samuel 17:5-6** also gives a description about Goliath, how tall he was and what he bore on his shoulders.

Both men spoken about in 1 Samuel were not a match to David because no matter how tall their shoulders were, God continues to look for something below the shoulders, something beyond human description, beyond what the eyes desire. God looks at the heart. His heartbeat goes beyond human comprehension. He said in the book of **Acts 13:22** *"I have found David the son of Jesse, a man after My own heart, who will do all my will"*.

This right here, is how God describes a son, he looks at the heart and ability to do his will.

That is why Jesus, facing the cross, uttered these words, "Nevertheless not my will but yours be done".

The shoulders spoken about in Isaiah 9 had already passed the heart test. Those were the humble shoulders ready to carry the government. The shoulders that were tried and tested and were found worthy.

Today I want to encourage you not to give up in your pruning season because the fruit you are about to become is for the benefit of the world. I actually like what **Romans 8:19** *says that creation is ` awaiting the manifestation of sons of man.*

There is someone, somewhere who is awaiting your shoulders to carry them through to the next level. Don't despair, whatever you are going through, Jesus went through it as well and he conquered it. You are more than a conqueror through Christ Jesus.

Yes, you can get through this, you can pull through it, nothing is impossible. Put your mind to it. Do it until you become it.

Chapter 2

RESPONSIBILITIES OF A SON

D uring the night <u>Paul</u> had a vision of a man of Macedonia standing and begging him, come over to Macedonia and help us" After Paul had seen the vision, <u>we</u> got ready at once to leave for Macedonia, concluding that God had called <u>us</u> to preach the gospel to them. Acts 16:9

I want you to notice a few things from this scripture. Paul was alone when he had a vision but immediately the vision was communicated to a team of disciples, they said WE must get ready to go and preach the gospel.

Beloved, it takes a team to preach the gospel, it takes people who believe in your vision to always be on standby to move with you. It takes real sons to run with your vision.

I like what Habakkuk said in **Habakkuk 2:2**

 And the Lord answered me, and said, "Write the vision, and make it plain upon tables, that he may run that readeth it."

Can you see now the purpose of a vision when it is written down that it is to be seen and something must happen? When a runner sees the vision he runs with it. Paul communicated the vision and instantly the runners were ready to run.

I actually like what they said, they said we must leave instantly to Macedonia. There were no questions asked, no element of doubt, just foot soldiers ready for the battle if and when the commander commands.

How many disciples still have an attitude like this today? In this day and age we live in an era, where everyone thinks they are called to the pulpit, where everyone is looking for his followers instead of following, where there are a lot of break-ups and breakaways in churches because of personal squabbles.

When you look at examples of Moses, Aaron and Joshua in the bible you get to see the true relationship of a visionary and vision runner.

This calls for the vision statement of your ministry.

You get to see how God called Moses aside whenever he wanted to speak to His nation and how the message was communicated through Moses to the Israelites.

One such example that comes to my spirit right now is in *Exodus 17:9*

And Moses said unto Joshua, Choose us out men and go out, fight with Amalek: tomorrow I will stand on the top of the hill with the rod of God in my hand.

10 So Joshua did as Moses had said to him and fought with Amalek: and Moses, Aaron and Hur went up to the top of the hill.

11 and it came to pass, when Moses held up his hand that Israel prevailed and when he let down his hand Amalek prevailed.

12 But Moses' hands were heavy and they took and put it under him and he sat thereon; and Aaron and Hur stayed up his hands, the one on one side, and the other on the other side; and his hands were steady until the going down of the sun.

I don't know if you saw the partnership in this passage? Yes, Moses was still the visionary but he knew that he cannot go to battle by himself. Can you see what happens when everyone takes their position? That will definitely make the world to become a better place.

Did you notice that Joshua didn't say to Moses, "why don't you go to the battlefield, do you want me to die? So you want me to go to the battlefield and you will be safe on some hill somewhere when I'm dead.

No, he simply did as Moses commanded. Later on, we also see how Moses' hands also got tired. Yes he was called, yes he was a visionary YET his hands got tired. So when that happened, members of his team came in and salvaged the situation. They became active participants. They didn't take over the rod from him and lifted it, they lifted his arms. They understood their role and position whilst they were with Moses.

Can you see how easy it gets when team players are occupying their rightful positions? You see the same pattern being followed in soccer matches where a goalkeeper stands in the same position of goalkeeping and defenders defend, goal scorers score, referees also do their work. There is no confusion in terms of positions, everyone knows where they are and what they should do.

A coach can look at an opportunity of a goal missed by his team but he cannot go inside and start playing. He can do all other stunts and shout but will remain in his position and awaits his turn to coach the team.

It is all about teamwork. Now let me ask a question, who is in your team? Are you a leader or a follower? If you are a leader, is there anyone following you? If you are a follower are you submissive to your leader? Are you supportive to your leader? Do you believe in what you are following? Are you following without asking any questions? In fact, until you are served, it is a sign that you should continue serving.

I like the last part of verse twelve where it says: "His hands were steady". Can you see what teamwork can do? On his own, his hands were tired but with the support of the team, his hands were steady.

My prayer today is that as believers our eyes of understanding can open up so that we can see the gospel truth of teamwork in our ministries and realize the roles that God has given to us to play and to play such roles truthfully and faithfully as unto the Lord.

Chapter 3

SONS ARE BORN WITH DEATH SENTENCES UPON THEIR LIVES

Then the king of Egypt said to the Hebrew midwives, of whom one was named Shiprah and the other Puah,

When you act as midwives to the Hebrew women and see them on the birthstool, if it is a <u>SON, YOU SHALL KILL HIM;</u> but if it's a daughter, she shall live.

But the midwives feared God and did not do as the king of Egypt commanded, but let the male babies live.

So the king of Egypt called for the midwives and said to them, Why have you done this thing and allowed the male children to live?

The midwives answered Pharaoh, "because the Hebrew women are not like the Egyptian women; they are vigorous and quickly delivered; their babies are born before the midwife comes to them."

So God dealt well with the midwives and the people multiplied and became very strong.

And because the midwives revered and feared God, he made them households (of their own)

Then Pharaoh charged all his people, saying, every son born (to the Hebrews) YOU SHALL CAST INTO THE RIVER (Nile) but every daughter you shall allow to live.

Exodus 1:15 – 22

What a decree this was! And we all know that when a King speaks, his words become law. From this passage of scripture, we can see a death sentence spoken upon every Hebrew son already. Are you one of those sons who was born amidst the controversy in your nation, city, village or household? Could it perhaps mean that your father denied responsibility when your mother announced that she was pregnant, or are you one of the children born in parts of our war-stricken Africa or even amid the AIDS pandemic where children outlive their parents or a survivor of abortion where both parents wanted to get rid of you for one reason or the other?

Either way, congratulations that you have made it this far and the truth is that all that happened to you is because of your purpose. Be of good cheer because you have conquered the very plan of the devil. You have won the battle against Satan himself. Your purpose and destiny shook him before you even landed.

Do you remember in the book of Genesis when God pronounced the enmity against the seed of the woman and the serpent? Yes, that is the destiny of sons being challenged right there. Your life matters a lot hence the level of attacks.

I want you to look back and check where God has taken you. Look at how far you made it. Take a good look at the battles, some of which you cannot even define or understand how you overcame them?

We serve a mighty God. He is the way maker, miracle worker, promise keeper and the deliverer. Nothing takes him by surprise. He remains the same January to December, he never changes in spite of every situation. His answer is yes and amen.

Right now I want to declare a Passover anointing upon you SON of God.

I want to declare null and void every pronouncement made by Pharaoh concerning your life. Every death sentence upon your life I declare an acquittal by the blood of the lamb.

I declare that the blood of Jesus paid the price in full. You will not be sentenced twice in Jesus's mighty name.

I declare that the blood of Jesus is speaking better things on your behalf right now.

Every plan and purpose that God pronounced into your spirit before you were born will come to pass in the name of Jesus.

I declare that you have a testimony about the bear and the lion that God delivered in your hand.

I declare that every uncircumcised Philistine is under your feet in the name of Jesus.

I declare a stone for every Goliath tormenting your life right now in the name of Jesus.

You are more than a conqueror in Christ Jesus. **Arise (from the depression and frustration in which circumstances have kept you – Arise to a new life! Shine (be radiant with the glory of the Lord), for your light has come, and the glory of the Lord has risen upon you. Isaiah 60:1** Amplified version. '

Chapter 4

FATHERS ARE A BLESSING TO THEIR SONS

The Lord said to Abram, go forth from your country,

And from your relatives

And from your father's house,

To the land which I will show you;

And I will make you a great nation,

And I will bless you, and make your name great;

And so you shall be a blessing;

And I will bless those who bless you, (emphasis me)

And the one who curses you I will curse.

And in you shall all the families of the earth be blessed. (emphasis me). Genesis 12:1

In this scripture, we see Father God preparing to bless Abram but we also see the blessing coming with some conditions.

We already saw in **Genesis 11:27** to **32** the biography and background of Abram.

Now God wants to bless Abram but he wants him to get out of his native country, out of the obvious and what he is used to so he can fully and completely be dependent upon God.

This made me to think about most believers today that God is actually calling them out of their comfort zone and they just like holding on to things that will delay us and not take us anywhere.

God was very clear to Abram over what he wanted him to do, but we see him doing the opposite. In fact as you continue reading, you will actually notice that, for as long as he didn't listen to the instruction, the promise never came to pass. As soon as God pronounced the blessing, the next thing we see is famine. As long as he is still with his father and cousin, no blessing manifested in his life.

What I draw from this passage is that, for as long as you are still in your father's house, he remains your head. God wanted to be the head in Abram's life and for as long as his biological father was there, God kept quite. God only began to speak and even changed his name after his father died and he was separated from his nephew Lot.

Yes he was rich and continued to be rich but was not blessed.

The bible tells us in **Proverbs 10:22** *that the blessing of the Lord maketh rich and addeth no sorrow to it.*

Can you see that it is not the riches that we need from God but the blessing and in that blessing there are riches without toiling? In Abram's riches, there was quarrelling between his shepherd and Lot's shepherd simply because God called Abram out not the whole family.

For as long as his father was with him, he didn't even go to where God directed him to go and nothing happened. After the father's death, there was still a cousin that he took along who also delayed the manifestation of the promises that God made to him.

Beloved I pray that as you know and are called by God, you will learn to hearken unto his voice and do exactly what he told you. I pray that every blessing that God has blessed you with can manifest in the natural. I pray for a quickening anointing upon every dream that is embedded in you.

Yes, God has blessed you but why is there no actual, tangible thing that you can testify about?

I urge you to look closely at your walk with God and to think back about the actual words that God spoke to you about.

Could it be that you have surrounded yourself with people that God wants you to cut out? Who is in your inner circle and what role are they playing towards your God given assignment? Are you pursuing what God has called and destined you to do or are you still surrounded by your relatives and cousins that God specifically has called you out of?

Beloved, do you remember Terah, Abram's father was an idolator (he worshipped idols) and perhaps the reason God wanted him out of the Ur of the Chaldees was to separate him from his background. In **Genesis 14:12** we also see how, after the separation, Lot, together with people at Sodom were taken over by other kings who fought against Sodom and then Abram had to go and rescue his nephew.

I am not suggesting that Abram should not have tried to rescue his nephew but you can see the kinds of detours and delays that we sometimes experience in life because we really like to do the opposite. In my opinion, if he just listened to what God said, this mission could have been accomplished earlier. I guess for as long as the human nature of feelings and affection is still in the driver's seat, the spiritual nature of taking after our spiritual father gets delayed. My prayer as I am writing now is that our spiritual nature can take over. **John 3:6** tells us that *Flesh gives birth to flesh and spirit gives birth to spirit.*

Could it be that when God wants to bless you, he first separates you from any kind of influence so that when you are blessed, you know that you know that all the glory belongs to him and him alone?

Let us take a sneak peek into the life of Joseph just to see how God separates before He blesses.

We see God making a promise to Joseph in a form of a dream. For as long as Joseph was still around his family, the promise remained in the womb. We only knew about the promise and there was no birthing to the promise until later on when he was sold to the Egyptians that the promise began to unfold.

The truth of the matter is that the blessing separates. God does not work with raw materials, He first separates, cleanses and once all the branches are purged and cut out, then he can use you.

Joseph's challenges started with his very close relatives, his family, the pit, the selling to the Egyptians, the accusations, the jail and eventually the second in command.

In all this, God only showed him the end results, he only saw his family bowing down to him through a dream but he was never shown how he will get to be second in command.

What I really like is his attitude whenever he was thrown into yet another challenge. He refused to stay there permanently. His attitude eventually determined his altitude.

It was through endurance, hard work and mostly keeping his faith in the promise that God gave him, that he conquered against all odds. Beloved, being a Joseph requires a lot more than you can imagine.

It does not come easy but the God that we serve always makes sure that in each part of the journey, he is always right there with you.

For Joseph's sake, Abraham had to sleep with Hagar to prepare the Ishmaelite's to buy Joseph at the right time to propel him to his destiny. One of the things that God always does is to prepare for your journey every step of the way. Without Hagar and Abraham, there would be no Ishmaelite's to purchase Joseph and take him to Egypt.

I just want to encourage someone right now that your journey to become the best has already been prepared, your transportation is already paid for in full, just believe in the God that has called you. The one who promised that though you walk through the fire it will not burn you, though you walk through the water you will not drown, he is still the same yesterday, today and forever more. Just trust in Him and He will surely give you the desires of your heart.

I know that we do not choose the place, the parents or relatives that we have but when God speaks and commands you out of where you presently are, it is not because they are bad people, it is because He remains a jealous God and He does not want to share His glory with anyone.

I believe if we can grasp this, the promises of God, which are 'Yes and Amen', will manifest in our lives faster than we can imagine.

I actually want to urge you to try and write down one of the instructions that God once spoke to you either through a prophecy, trance or dream and go and check if there was any instruction directly given to you and just check whether you followed it to the latter.

Proverbs 4:1 puts it this way,

Hear, o sons, the instruction of the father, and give attention that you may gain understanding. **(New American Standard bible)**

Proverbs 4:1

Hear, my sons, the instruction of a father, and pay attention, in order to gain and to know intelligent discernment, comprehension and interpretation (of spiritual matters) (**Amplified version**)

I like using different versions of the bible so that I get a better understanding of a passage. The above scripture, when amplified, gives a broader meaning of what instructions do. It says it gives you a better interpretation of spiritual matters. For as long as you still want to interpret spiritual matters in the natural way, you will carry your father and cousin on a trip that requires only you. Moreover, as I said, God is not saying your father is bad; he just wants you all to himself.

Furthermore, being under your father's roof will also mean that there will be two competing voices, that of your father and the voice of God.

We also see competing voices with Gideon who was called by God to be a mighty warrior yet he was afraid to deal with the father's altar. When two voices are competing, chances are that you will listen to one and not the other. The bible makes it very clear that you cannot serve two masters.

We saw it with Moses that whenever God wanted to speak to the nation of Israel, he called Moses aside and gave him instructions. Therefore, I can gladly conclude that one of God's *modus operandi* is separating you from the complacency of your comfort zone to give you specific instructions.

Genesis 14:14-15 (King James Version)

14 And the Lord said unto Abram, after that Lot was separated from him, lift up now thine eyes, and look from the place where thou art northward, and southward, and eastward and westward.

15 for all the land which thou seest, to thee I will give it, and to thy seed forever.

The New American Standard Version puts it this way, **The Lord said to Abram, after Lot had separated from him, NOW lift up your eyes and look from the place where you are,**

northward and southward and eastward and westward, for all the land which you see, I will give it to you and to your descendants forever.

Can you see that God still kept his first promise, he just kept quiet until everyone is gone? I intentionally put the capital letters on "now" just to emphasize that God was just saying, it is time to work now that I have your full attention.

Before Lot and Abram were separated, God said no word about the land he wanted to give to Abram forever. From this, I can actually say that the quickest way to see the manifestation of God's promises in your life is to remain separated as you get the instructions that will make the blessing to rest upon you forever.

Who, in their right mind can say no to forever? Who can say no to a blessing that will overflow to generations to come?

Let us get wisdom from this and access our blessing according to the promise from our father. He has good plans for us. Plans to prosper us and not to harm us. Can you see that prosperity is one of the plans that God has already planned for you? It is not an accident that you are prosperous; it is part of the plan by your father.

Now let us look at other scriptures and how the blessing was imparted from fathers to sons.

Genesis 25:5

And Abraham gave all what he had to Isaac. **(Amplified**)

Abraham left everything he owned to Isaac. *(NIV Version)*

After everything has been given, what else is left? Absolutely nothing. Yes, Abraham had other sons, seven sons to be exact but he gave them gifts, but to the son of promise he gave everything. I mean everything.

The book of **Proverbs 13:22** says *a good man leaves an inheritance (of moral stability and goodness) to his children's children, and the wealth of the sinner (finds its way eventually)* into the hands of the righteous, for whom it was laid up.

Can you see that this inheritance by fathers must actually outlive the sons and go to the grand children as well? It is pressed down and overflowing to the next generation. That is the kind of abundance only our God has planned for us.

Genesis 27:1

And it came to pass, that when Isaac was old and his eyes were dim, so that he could not see, he called Esau his eldest son, and said unto him, my son, and he said unto him, behold, here I am.

And he said, behold now, I am old, I know not the day of my death:

Now, therefore take I pray thee, thy weapon, thy quiver and thy bow, and go out to the field and take me some venison:

And make me savoury meat, such as I love and bring it to me, that I may eat; THAT MY SOUL MAY BLESS THEE BEFORE I DIE.

Other versions say **SO THAT I MAY GIVE YOU MY BLESSING BEFORE I DIE.**

Can you see that inside every father there is a blessing to leave to his sons?

It takes a father to bless, it takes a father to leave a blessing, it takes a father to speak a blessing upon his children and we continue to see it happening throughout the bible.

Genesis 49:1

Then Jacob called for his sons and said: "gather around so I can tell you what will happen to you in days to come.

Assemble and listen, sons of Jacob: listen to your father Israel.

We all know that Israel was Jacob's spiritual name meaning father of nations. We just learnt in chapter 48 that Jacob was actually sick and knew that he is about to die. You see, he knows that he has a blessing that he must release to his sons hence he summoned them. The natural Jacob was sick and weak but Israel was about to address the sons. When he summoned his sons, he gathered them in the natural to give them spiritual instructions of things to come. Israel blessed his sons.

Genesis 48

And it came to pass after these things, that one told Joseph, behold thy father is sick, and he took with him two sons, Manasseh and Ephraim.

And one told Jacob, and said, behold, thy son Joseph cometh unto thee: and Israel strengthened himself and sat upon the bed.

And Jacob said unto Joseph, God Almighty appeared unto me at Luz in the land of Canaan, and blessed me,

And said unto me, Behold, I will make thee fruitful, and multiply thee, and I will make of thee a multitude of people, and will give this land to thy seed after thee for an everlasting possession.

Now, thy two sons, Ephraim and Manasseh that were born unto thee in the land of Egypt before I came unto thee into Egypt, ARE MINE; as Reuben and Simeon, they shall be mine.

From this scripture, we can see that Israel wanted to bless the sons of Joseph as his own but before the blessing; they had to be sons first.

Fathers gives blessings to sons. To this day, the 12 tribes of Israel had half tribe of Ephraim and Manasseh and there was no tribe of Joseph. I once heard that in the Jewish tradition, fathers take time every Friday to speak blessings over their children. No wonder the Jewish people are very few yet among the richest in the world. Perhaps one can learn and practice a blessing that the bible speaks about in the book of proverbs that it maketh rich and addeth no sorrow. Fathers have this endowed blessing within them that as they speak, it cometh to pass.

If I can take Reuben as a case study from **Genesis 49:3-4** that states that:
Reuben, thou art my firstborn,
My might, and the beginning of my strength,
Thy Excellency of dignity and the Excellency of power. Unstable as water, thou shalt not excel because thou wentest up to thy father's

bed, then defilest thou it, he went up to my couch.

As a father, Jacob is telling his son what will happen to him because of what he once did. He is saying that his son will not excel in life. In other words he is saying the opposite of what a blessing does and as we continue reading the bible, we see how his words came to pass until another father, which I will call a father in the Lord (Moses) reversed it. In the book of **Deutoronomy 33:6** he said "__Let the tribe of Reuben live and not die__.

Reuben was destined not to excel and it took another father to speak into his life for things to change or to take a different direction. I chose this case study just to show the power of the blessing by the father to sons. Furthermore to emphasize the importance of words spoken to our children.

I would further like to bring to the fathers attention the power of the tongue. Some fathers, sometimes out of anger, disappointment or in the spur of the moment have spoken words that became seeds of destruction to their children.

Remember that there is always an angel ready to perform and carry out that word. The Bible tells us that angels are ministering on our behalf, so it is very important to speak positively upon our children at all times.

Sons take the vision of their fathers to the next level. David, a man after god's heart, gathered the gold then Solomon used it to build God's temple.

1Kings 5:3

You know how David my father could not build a house to the name of the Lord his God because wars were about him on every side until the Lord put his foes under his feet.

Jesus, the son of God, finally dealt with a long outstanding problem. The water problem during Moses' time, Moses used a rod to part the water, Joshua stepped in the water to enter the Promised Land then Jesus, the King of Kings and Lord of Lords walked on the water. He put the long outstanding problem under his feet forever.

Beloved, what is it that has been a thorn in your flesh? What has been bothering you from one generation to the other? Jesus is the solution to the problem. The son of man has conquered it forever.

Matthew 22:44

The lord said to my lord, sit at my right hand until I put your enemies under your feet?

There is one place where your enemies belong to, that is under your feet. Now is the time to walk above every principality and powers that challenge your destiny. This is a promise by the son of God, to put the enemy right where he belongs. Arise and walk above as a son of God.

1Corinthians 15:25-28

For Christ must be King and reign until he has put all His enemies under his feet. The last enemy to be subdued and abolished is death.

For he (The Father) has put all things in subjection under His (Christ's) feet. But when it says, all things are put to subjection (under him), it is evident that he (Himself) is exempted who does the subjecting of all things to Him.

However, when everything is subjected to him, then the son himself will also subject himself to (the father) who put all things under him, so that God may be all in all (be everything to everyone, supreme, the indwelling and controlling factor of life).

The last verse says it all. When everything is subjected to the son of God, it stays under the feet forever. May you walk on top of everything that has been walking on top of you by the power of the risen son of God?

Chapter 5

OBSTACLES ALONG THE BIRTHING OF SONS

I just want to share a few biblical truths about sons who were born and the obstacles they conquered.

In one of the previous chapters, I shared about the life of Moses which I will not be repeating here but suffices to say that when you are called by God, definitely the kingdom of darkness would try by all means to abort the greatness and calling upon your life.

Perhaps as you are reading this chapter, you are one of the people whose mother went through difficulties, obstacles, and challenges, etc. just for you to be here today. If you are, I would like to say cheer up, the best is yet to come, and you have already conquered the devil. Put on your best shoes and dance a victory dance.

Let us now look into a few of such sons and what they overcame.

1 Samuel 1:1

Now there was a certain man of Ramathaim-zophim, of mount Ephraim, and his name was Elkanah, the son of Zuph, an Ephradite:

And he had two wives, the name of the one was Hannah and the name of the other Peninah: and Peninah had children but Hannah had no children.

And this man went up out of his city yearly to worship and to sacrifice unto the Lord of hosts in Shiloh. And the two sons of Eli, Hophni and Phinehas, the priests of the Lord were there.

And when the time was that Elkanah offered, he gave to Peninah his wife, and to all her sons and her daughter's portions.

But unto Hannah he gave a worthy portion, for he loved Hannah: but the Lord had shut up her womb.

And her adversary also provoked her sore, for to make her fret, because the Lord had shut up the womb.

And as he did so year by year, when she went up to the house of the Lord, so she provoked her, therefore she wept, and did not eat.

Then said Elkanah her husband to her, Hannah why weepest thou? And why eatest thou not? And why is thy heart grived? Am not I better to thee than ten sons?

So Hannah rose up after they had eaten in Shiloh, and after they had drunk. Now Eli the priest sat upon a seat by a post of the temple of the Lord.

And she was in bitterness of soul, and prayed unto the Lord, and wept sore.

And she vowed a vow, and said, o Lord of hosts, if thou wilt indeed look on the affliction of thine handmaid, and remember me, and not forget thine handmaid, but wilt give unto thine handmaid a MAN CHILD (my emphasis) then I will give him unto the Lord all the days of his life, and there shall no razor come upon his head.

I just want to draw your attention to a few things mentioned in this scripture. My first comment will be on the emptiness that Hannah felt without a child. The love of the husband combined could not quench the desire of her womb to carry a son. Whatever the husband did, could not substitute the burning desire from within.

Beloved, there are certain things only God can fill you to the fullest. You may be one of the people perhaps staying in a mansion, driving the latest top of the range car, staying in an exclusive suburban by the beachfront with a bank account of infinite zeros yet feeling or going through what Hannah went through.

I am here to encourage you that all women in the bible who were to carry or deliver greatness of sons went through barrenness. Therefore, I just want to encourage you today that your womb will carry and give birth to greatness despite whatever plan your enemy has in store for you.

I actually loved the use of the word adversary in verse 6. It reminded me of **1 Peter 5:8** that says: *"Be sober, be vigilant; because of your adversary the devil, as a roaring lion, walketh about, seeking whom he may devour."*

Now you can see that the devil had a representative in the form of Peninah. Whatever she did was to make sure that Hannah will be hurt and will cry. Can you see the tactic used by the enemy here? As you shed some tears he will keep on hurting you, the enemy is out to get you, he is aiming for your jugular vein yet you are still massaging him.

As a woman, I can identify a lot with the Peninah types. I know how "we" sometimes can dress in a particular way to send a particular statement without uttering a word or walk a certain walk that will send the message to whomever the victim might be in silence. So I was just picturing in my mind how Peninah would start calling his children one by one, loudly to make sure that Hannah can hear as she was about to give them their offering. I can picture how she just rubbed it in her every time Hannah was to send her children to the shop in summer that she would perhaps call back her child and tell Hannah to go by herself and not send the children in the scorching sun or maybe, whenever she missed her periods she would make such a big deal out of it and want Hannah to be the first one to know.

I am just thinking aloud because I know in 9 out of 10 cases where another woman is hurting or in pain is mainly because of another woman somewhere, somehow. At least now, we know that the bible calls them adversaries and as long as you are still crying, you are still very far from your freedom.

I want you to note that Hannah AROSE (my emphasis) and did something different. Not only did she pray but also she made a vow.

Beloved, there are times and circumstances where you have to change your tactics and arise. Daughter of Zion, arise and shine. When your adversary is up against you, you have a weapon with your mouth and tongue. Begin to speak to your God, your creator.

Be specific with your request, we have learned from this scripture that Hannah did not just ask for a baby or a child. She was specific, she wanted a man-child not a baby boy but a man-child. Such children are born out of hard work, out of adversity, out of turmoil, out of opposition but when you synchronize your mouth, knees, and womb, a man-child will come out. It does not matter how barren you are, if you must give birth to purpose and significance, it will overcome.

I just want to encourage you today that whatever you are going through, God knows it and a prayer coupled with a vow can give birth to what you confess.

Can you see how the power of confession gave birth to Prophet Samuel? God gave this one weapon unto us from the foundation of the earth when he called everything into creation by the word.

What kind of words are you uttering to yourself today? What kind of confessions are you making with your mouth? It is about time the words become flesh in your life. The bible says that life and death is in the power of the tongue. Go ahead and use that power. You are empowered by God to succeed, to prosper, to make it, to be on top.

Mark 11:23 says, **For verily, I say unto you, that whosoever shall say unto this mountain, be thou removed, and be thou cast into the sea; and shall not doubt in his heart, that shall believe that those things which he saith shall come to pass, he shall have whatsoever she saith.**

There we go; this passage clearly explains how to deal with adversities of life. It calls such challenges, mountains and it further explains that mountains bow to 'sayings'.

Mountains respond to 'sayings'. Whatsoever thing you do not want, say it and it is as good as gone.

Right now, I would like to challenge you to think of a mountain in front of you, I want you to begin to speak to the mountain. I want you to open your mouth and address the mountain. I want you to **say** it and believe every word that you are saying and see the mountain melting in front of you. The God that we serve is bigger than the mountain in front of you. He is bigger than the valley you are going through.

In addition, in his word he promised us that though we walk through the valley of the shadow of death, we should fear no evil. When you are in the valley, as you are speaking you are walking. Oh! What an awesome God we serve! He already knew the mountain and the valley long before you even came to it and he has already provided the answer to your problem. There is nothing new under the sun indeed.

Just going back to Hannah's experience, we can see that her ordeal was actually aimed at preventing the greatest prophet to be born but more so that the prophet who was to anoint among others, king David. From this, you can see how the adversary goes out of his way to prevent the lineage, the future significant leaders to be born.

Only if our noses could do better than just smelling, but really smell into the future and know exactly what the adversary is up to. Can you imagine what could have happened if Hannah gave up and decided to do nothing about it? Can you see how far the enemy goes to try to destabilize your future generation?

My prayer for you today is that you should indeed be alert, be vigilant towards your adversary. If someone is tormenting you in a certain area, ask yourself a question, what is it that he is preventing me to achieve? Perhaps your boss at work is tormenting you despite the good job that you are doing, could it be that he is afraid of you taking over and doing far much better than what he is doing. It is not in every situation that you should give up. Speak to the mountain and see what happens.

Another son born out of adversity and trial was Isaac. Isaac was born at a time when Sarah had given up and even her age was speaking a different language when it comes to giving birth. She was at her old age, the husband was old and she had already decided to become God's helper and arranged a concubine for her husband but God kept his promise against all odds. Isaac had to come from the womb of Sarah at the appointed time.

As if that was not enough, God had to come back and test Abraham with the very son that he just blessed him with by asking him to be offered as a sacrifice. You know just reading this gives me goose bumps. I cannot even put myself in Sarah's situation. This can be one test that I will dismally fail. But out of that test, there is a better testimony. From that mess of arranging a concubine into a message that God never fails.

Beloved can you look at the situation you are in now and fast forward it to the celebration that lies ahead. Can you see the beauty that will come out of the ashes you are experiencing now Praise God that He is not a man that he should lie. Whatever he says comes to pass, whatever he promises will surely come to pass.

Imagine the situation with Rachel and Leah. Imagine how from the beginning Rachel, though loved by Jacob, spent most of her time in a childless marriage when her sister and concubines kept on bearing children. Imagine what could have been going on in her mind for years. Imagine the prayers she prayed.

We later understood why she had to go through that when she gave birth to Joseph and Benjamin and how those two children revolutionized the bible, as we know it today. Her womb was destined to carry the future vice president of Egypt hence she was attacked by the adversary the way she did. The pain, the humiliation, the waiting, the discouragement, all that so that her womb would fail to produce the fruit it was destined to birth.

I do not know what you are going through right now but I can tell you that it is never about you. The greater the destiny, the greater the attack. Whatever you are enduring right now is because of the future you are carrying. Get up, walk tall and know that all things worketh together for your greater good. God is perfecting you to become what you should become. God does not use people without experience, he doesn't call the qualified, he calls and qualifies you. He did it with Moses and he is doing it with you. He is still in the business of building future generation of sons.

Lastly let us look at the king of kings, the son of God and what the parents went through. Right now I imagine the challenges that comes through pregnancy. The morning sickness, the fatigue, backache, mood swings, etc. For a second I want to picture Mary, pregnant and having to take a trip in that era where there were no cars, aeroplanes, business class and you have to be at the back of a donkey for days in a scorching desert sun and travel to a different place because what you are carrying is under siege. Imagine a number of children who had to be killed because of Jesus.

Woman arise and perceive the greatness you are carrying. Arise and smell the coffee. There is greatness in you. Dig deep within you and find out what is inside of you. When Adam could not find a companion amongst different animals presented to him, he looked within himself, and right there, by his rib was his companion. Praise God Hallelujah I'm so excited just writing this right now? And I say YES to the greatness within me. Yes to the calling upon my life. Yes to the favor that God has favoured me with.

The angel said to Mary. Blessed art thou amongst women, I say to you, blessed art thou amongst women. The same measure of blessings that Mary received is upon you. Our God is the same yesterday, today and forevermore and he doesn't change. Open your mouth and receive this blessing right now in the name of Jesus. Confess it until you see the manifestations in the name of Jesus.

Chapter 6

IMPRISONED GREATNESS

I was watching a documentary on TV about male prisoners/ inmates when the Holy Spirit deposited this in my heart. I observed closely and realized that most of the inmates were talented in different ways. There were those who sang, others played guitars, etc.

I began to think deeply about these men, not as inmates but as careers of greatness. I began to have compassion just realizing the plan of the enemy concerning their lives. I began to think of future children imprisoned in their loins and charged with a crime they did not commit.

We all know that for a son/child to be born, you need a seed of a man. Just like God in the book of Genesis 1:2b says that **the spirit of God was moving (hovering, brooding) over the face of the waters. 3 And God said, let there be light, and there was light.**

I will make an analogy of the face of the waters to the womb and the word that God spoke in verse 3 as the seed because we know that the word of God is a seed. When this word was spoken, it birthed light.

Going back to the documentary, I began to realize that these prisoners, guilty or not, some of them if not most are in a spiritual prison than physical. Let me explain what I mean. I believe that there are people who are carriers of greatness and that the enemy looked ahead into their future and devised a plan to curb the greatness.

To give a direct biblical example will be to use Joseph, who from an early age through dreams knew that he was destined for greatness and he shared his dream with his immediate family hoping that they would celebrate him. To his surprise, his brothers became his instant enemies. They went to an extent of selling him to foreigners and hoped that they will kill the dream that he had. The persecutions never stopped, he was further accused and imprisoned in Egypt all because of that divine greatness that he carried along with him.

The enemy never stopped operating because he was in prison. You see, when the enemy is after you, he goes for the jugular vein, he aims for the kill, he wants to finish you off. He will even use those closest to you to accomplish his evil plan. He will use corrupt officials to bury you deep into the crime you did not commit, he will use false witnesses and plant false evidence to support the crime.

In essence, what I'm saying is that you might be reading this book and you are in prison, and you also know that you are accused of something you did not do, in other words, you are framed to protect someone greater in authority or society. I have got news for you.

All that is happening to you is because of what you carry inside of you. Your seed is under siege. You are a carrier of great men and women on your loins. The enemy is trying to distort and disturb you from what you must launch out. Be courageous, do not dismay for God is with you.

Genesis 45:3-4

And Joseph said to his brothers, I am Joseph! Is my father still alive? And his brothers could not reply, for they were distressingly disturbed and dismayed at (the startling realization that they were in) his presence.

4. And joseph said to his brothers, come near to me, I pray you, and they did so, and he said, I am Joseph your brother, whom you sold to Egypt!

5 But now, do not be distressed and disheartened or vexed or angry with yourselves because you sold me here, for God sent me ahead of you to preserve life.

Oh wow, can you see what happens when God separates you from your accusers? Can you see the ultimate attitude that Joseph had? Not a trace or element of revenge at all. He actually displayed the forgiveness that only the heart of God can display. He saw his assignment from God as the only thing that he had to do to achieve what God had planned for him. Can you see that at times what you are going through is not actually for yourself? When you are called and appointed, certain things that you are going through and the enemy is challenging you not to achieve is for the greatness you carry.

When you are a carrier of greatness, God takes care of everything. It may look like a conundrum at first but to God it is a straight line. For Joseph, God took care of his transportation to Egypt long before he was born. It was through Abraham and Hagar that the Ishmalites tribe was born, the very Ishmalites who bought Joseph from his brothers and later sold him to Potiphar. In God's eyes, Joseph's dream was meant to come to pass. The transportation, the prison, the throne, all was God's plan. So, whatever you are going through, God has a plan for you. Relax, be still and know that he is God.

If I am to bring this closer to home, I will give an example of a great South African icon who ever lived. His name was Nelson Rolihlahla Mandela. A man of great stature and integrity. A man who like other inmates reading this book now was thrown into prison to stop the president inside of him. When he was released, he became the first black South African president who wanted peace, stability, integrated and non-racial South Africa. He did not come out to revenge those who threw him in jail, he came out full of love and forgiveness and that was the legacy he left for us as South Africans and the human race in general.

Basically what I'm saying is that look deep within yourself and you will find answers. All that is happening is not about you. It's not about who you are, it's about whose you are. Take some time off, think back, think deep, look inside yourself with a microscope. What were your desires, plans, dreams, and aspirations before you were imprisoned? What was your bigger plan? Could it be that it is God's plan that has put you behind bars? Could it be that it is God's plans that are locked in and not you? Could it be that if there was a way of separating your greatness from you, you will be set free tomorrow?

Again I'm saying, be courageous, Jesus overcame, so shall you. Joseph overcame, so shall You. Your expectation shall not be cut off. You are more than a conqueror through Christ Jesus. He paid the price in full. Hang in there, your day of victory is coming. Come on, practice your victory dance. Your mind cannot be imprisoned, your dreams cannot be imprisoned and they can still be realized. The very people who imprisoned you will come to seek your wisdom. You are a great man of God. The greatest seed of Abraham. A carrier of God's display of greatness. You are blessed.

Chapter 7

EXPOSURE TO THE SON WILL PREVENT BURNING

***A**nd God said, let there be lights in the firmament of the heaven to divide the day from the night; and let them be for signs, and for seasons, and for days, and years.*

And let them be for lights in the firmament of the heaven to give light upon the earth and it was so.

And God made two great lights in the firmament of the heaven to give light upon the earth, the lesser light to rule the night, he made the stars also. Genesis 1:14-16

From this passage, we can notice the different lights that God created and their purpose but I just want to dwell on the lesser and greater light which is the sun and the moon.

As I was researching and meditating on the comparison of the sun and the moon, I discovered the following. The moon does not have the light of its own. The light we see from the moon is the light of the sun reflected toward Earth. When you see the phases of the moon, you are only seeing part of the moonlighted surface because at any time exactly half of its surface is facing the sun and receiving the light from it. With a telescope, you can dimly see the part that is not lighted because some light from the earth is likewise being reflected to the moon.

Now that we have seen where the moon gets its light, it reminds me of the scripture in John

8:28 that says that: *"**Then said Jesus unto them, when ye have lifted up the Son of man, then shall ye know that I am He, and that I do nothing of myself, but as my father hath taught me, I speak these things.**"*

If we are to take this analogy and see God as the greater light and Jesus as the lesser light, we will then get the revelation that Jesus as the "moon" is fully dependant on the sun to provide Him with light, so is Jesus depending and doing only what God instructs him to do.

I just want to emphasize that this is only a comparison and that I am in no way trying to say that Jesus is the moon and God is the sun and people who worship the sun or the moon will in any way begin to quote or rather misquote my example. This is just an analogy and God is still the creator of everything and worshipping the creation instead of the creator is totally against his plans. Every knee should still bow to him and him alone as the CREATOR.

I also want to bring to your attention Genesis 1:3 that, the light was already created and divided from darkness and that the light that we speak about in verse 13 was for a specific purpose and that was for rulership. Verse 18 specifically says that it was to rule over the day and the night, and to divide the light from darkness and God saw that it was good.

Let me take you ahead to the famous scripture in Isaiah 9:6 which states that for unto us a child is born, unto us a son is given and the government shall be upon his shoulders.

Can you see from this that the son came to rule and reign? Can you see that from the beginning Jesus was born as a King to rule and reign on earth? Can you see the greatest plan of God upon his sons is rulership? The book of Psalms put it this way, it says the Lord shall send the rod of thy strength out of Zion: Rule thou in the midst of thine enemies. This continues to show that it is the Lord that sends the rod or sceptre for the son to rule. Do you remember the rod that Moses used to deliver the Israelites from the red sea and the Egyptians? It is the same rod of rulership, the sceptre of kingship, a sceptre to be the head and not the tail, a sceptre for the kingdom of God to come down. That is why when Jesus was teaching the disciples how to pray, he mentioned the kingdom of God that must come down. It is on this earth that sons must rule and reign. It is on this earth that the kingdom of heaven must come down and it is the sons that are ready to carry the kingdom or the government upon their shoulders.

This task is not for the faint-hearted neither is it for the disobedient because a true son only reflects what the father is instructing and does what he sees the father doing. This trumpet that we are sounding through this book is for the sons to arise and take over their positions.

Romans 8:19 from the amplified version says: *"For (even the whole) creation (all nature) waits expectantly and longs earnestly for God's sons to be made known (waits for the revealing, the disclosing of their son ship."* The King James Version says: *"for the earnest expectation of the creature waitheth the manifestation of sons of God."*

Are you ready to manifest the rulership that God has called you to? All you have to say is "Yes" then do the rest. Remember that when a prince is born, he doesn't have to do anything to become a king. He is born with royal blood and he just await his turn to rule. When the wise men from the east were preparing to go and see Jesus, the bible tells us that they were following a star to see a king that was born. He didn't announce or broadcast it anywhere but the astronomers picked it from the kind of star that they saw. The blood was royal though he was born in a stable. Nothing could change who he was.

I want to say the same thing about you. The bible calls you the royal priesthood which means you are born with the crown upon your head. You are a son of a king born to rule in the midst of your enemies. You are born to carry the government upon your shoulders. The question is, are you ready to take that responsibility? Are you ready to reign? Creation is awaiting you. Heaven was a witness when you were born, there is a star out there that marked the day you were born, and you were born for this. All you have to do is to trust God and believe that you have a purpose right here on earth. It is to believe that certain things or people will not be liberated until you take your position.

For the Persians it was Esther, for the Israelites it was Moses and Joshua, Samson, Daniel, Shardrack, Meshack and Abednigo.

Begin to see yourself in the picture, who are you and what is your role in God's big picture? Are you a supporting role player or the main character? Whichever you are, take position and possession of what God has called you to do. You are not a mistake but a royal priesthood. You are not the circumstances that you were born under. Like I said about Jesus that being born in a stable did not change his royal status so whether your parents rejected you or threw you in a bin to be rescued by a passer-by is a sure case that you are born to rule.

You are a lion of the tribe of Judah. Just as the lion is the king of the jungle, so are you and no matter how the circumstances can change in the jungle, a lion never eats grass because it is a carnivore. It knows its identity without doubt and it is not apologetic. Embrace your kingship and be what God says you are in Jesus's name.

Chapter 8

THE SPIRIT OF THE FATHER

Noah began to be a man of the soil, and he planted a vineyard. He drank of the wine and became drunk and lay uncovered in his tent. And Ham, the father of canaan, saw the nakedness of his father and told his two brothers outside. Then Shem and Japheth took a garment, laid it on both their shoulders, and walked backward and covered the nakedness of their father. Their faces were turned backward, and they did not see their father's nakedness when Noah woke from his wine and knew what his youngest son had done to him, he said *"cursed be Canaan; a servant of servants shall he be to his brothers.* **Genesis 9:20**

Noah had three sons namely, Ham, Shem and Japheth. Ham was the youngest of the sons of Noah and he saw the nakedness of his father when Noah (the father) was drunk.

Ham, being the youngest was also immature and irresponsible. Sonship requires a level of responsibility to always protect the nakedness of the father. Because of Ham's actions, the blessings of Canaan, the grandchildren of Ham were cursed.

Shem and Japheth took the garment and laid it on their **shoulders** as an action to cover the nakedness of their father. This secured them their father's blessing.

Beloved, over and above what is mentioned on this scripture, I just want to remind you that God had already blessed Noah and his sons hence the curse upon Ham went to Canaan. That is a discussion for another day but suffice to say that what God had already blessed, cannot be cursed.

Numbers 11:16

Then the Lord said to Moses," Gather for me seventy men of the elders of Israel, whom you know to be the elders of the people and officers over them, and bring them to the tent of meeting, and let them take their stand there with you. And i will come down and talk with you there. And I will take some of the spirit that is in you and put it on them, and they shall bear the burden of the people with you, so that you may not bear it yourself alone.

It is THE HEART BEAT of every father for his sons to have His spirit (the spirit of the father). When God in Heaven saw that the burden over the shoulders of Moses his servant was too heavy for him, He wanted to lighten the burden and responsibilities of Moses. The key on this is what God does to lighten the burden. God said, **"I will take some of the Spirit that is in you and put it on them"**. It is important for us to understand, for a son to cover and protect the nakedness of his father, he must also have the **spirit of his father**.

The emphasis here is that God did not put His spirit on the seventy leaders, but He took the same spirit that was in Moses and put it on the leaders to alleviate burden upon Moses. It was only after they got the spirit of Moses that they functioned like Moses. It is important for sons to have the spirit of the father.

2Kings 2:9 (NIV) says, **when they had crossed, Elijah said to Elisha, "Tell me what can I do for you before I am taken from you?"**

"Let me inherit a double portion of your spirit" Elisha replied.

The Amplified version says, **"Let a double portion of your spirit be upon me.**

In conclusion, as we study about the spirit of the father, we learnt that indeed Elijah said that Elisha has asked for a hard thing but nevertheless we learnt that as Elijah was taken, Elisha cried out in a loud voice calling upon his father Elijah and the cloak of Elijah fell upon Elisha.

From this chapter we further learn that a group of prophets who were standing at a distance, observed how Elisha parted the river with the mantle of Elijah and they said, "surely the spirit of Elijah is upon Elisha.

We also learnt that Elisha, in his lifetime performed twice as many miracles as his father Elijah.

I could not conclude this book without talking about the spirit of a father upon his son without writing about the relationship of this two. Elisha asked for a double portion of the anointing upon his father and he got exactly that. What I learnt from this is that indeed the father will never withhold whatever the son is requesting.

As Elijah was taken, I want you to notice that throughout the scriptures, Elisha referred to Elijah as his master and as soon as he got the revelation of him as the father and shouted, "my father, my father", the cloak fell.

There is a blessing in the revelation of who your father is. There is also a blessing that only sons can receive from their father. We saw this with Abraham, when he was to ascent Mount Moria that his servants had to stay behind and he ascended with his son. There are places only sons can go to with their father which servants cannot go to.

We continue to see the heartbeat of the father towards his sons throughout the book. It is in the heartbeat of the father for sons to takeover, to stay connected to the source, to have his spirit, to bring the kingdom of heaven on earth. It is also His heartbeat to protect, to bless and to release His sons to manifest throughout His creation.

Galatians 3:28-29 says: There is neither Jew nor Greek, there is neither slave nor free, there is neither male nor female; for you are all one in Christ Jesus. And if you are Christ's, then you are Abraham's seed, and heirs according to the promise. And indeed, Abraham's blessings is ours.

Dedication

This book is dedicated to two people posthumously. Their impact in my life will remain engraved in my heart forever.

To my Apostle, dear friend and father of Divine Harvest Ministries International Theo Mankga, your death was very painful and unexpected but the pain propelled me to finish this book.

Thank you again for coming through for me to bury my grand-mother, only for you to depart a year later.

And to Bophelo Matete Nong "äka" the Champ, you are simply the best. You gave me a 30 days roller coaster ride that will last me a lifetime.

May your dearest souls rest in eternal peace, I love you tons.

To Moruti Johny Lebogo, your contribution is immensely appreciated, the pushing was not nice but finally we made it to the end. Thank you for displaying true sonship and for tireless prayers throughout.

To my family and friends, thank you for believing in me and the calling that God has called me and for the encouragement. You are my fortress and strength always.

We would like to hear from you, please connect with us on the following social media handles:

+27 82 593 9248

Kholofelo Kolanisi